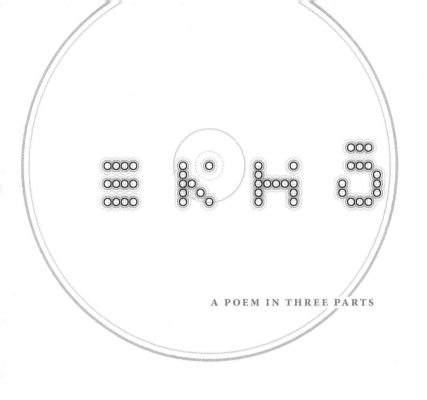

ECHO

A POEM IN THREE PARTS

Roslyn Orlando

Soft Skull New York

EKHŌ

First Soft Skull edition: 2025

Library of Congress Cataloging-in-Publication Data
Names: Orlando, Roslyn, author.
Title: Ekhō : a poem in three parts / Roslyn Orlando.
Description: First Soft Skull edition. | New York : Soft Skull, 2025. |
    Includes bibliographical references.
Identifiers: LCCN 2024044204 | ISBN 9781593767983 (trade paperback) |
    ISBN 9781593767990 (ebook)
Subjects: LCGFT: Poetry.
Classification: LCC PR9619.4.O75 E34 2025 | DDC 821.91—dc23/
    eng/20241008
LC record available at https://lccn.loc.gov/2024044204

Cover design by Farjana Yasmin
Cover art: lattice mountain © Roslyn Orlando;
holographic terrain © iStock / Kittiphat Abhiratvorakul
Book design by tracy danes

Soft Skull Press
New York, NY
www.softskull.com

Printed in the United States of America

10 9 8 7 6 5 4 3 2 1

Camille,
for reading with me

One thing about hell is the echo is fabulous.

ANNE CARSON, "Good Dog"

Contents

PART 1   1

PART 2   29

PART 3   53

Notes   81
Acknowledgments   85

PART

Prologue

1. Ekhō began with a body—
arms, legs, knuckles, trachea
spoke garrulously like a drunk
politician (better intentions
but still), sometimes annoying,
a smile like corn.

2. The other nymphs who hung
out on the sloped mountains of Boeotia
early commune of free love
thought Ekhō benignly entertaining
(she was invited to dinners
but not to séances).

3. Zeus, all puffed up, was not
good at many things except for
getting his way. Hera, his wife,
was even more skilled in this
department. No matter.
On nice days he commonly wanted
to have sex with the mountain nymphs.
He would descend from the heavens
on his gentle winged horse to flirt
and do those other things.
He justified these indiscretions
with a pagan relish for tradition
disguised as morality—a trick taught
to him by mortals.

4.   The nymphs were ambivalent
toward his large thunderbolts
but feigned admiration, pleased and
were pleased for a few hours away
from their own daily chores, tending
to the juniper, myrtle, oleander, cypress.

5.   With subscription to
the rumorous wind, Hera,
jealous avenger of infidelity
came looking.

6.   Ekhō, with talent for idle chatter
was sent to stall her; to muse
on the price of grain, indulge in
gossip of the local oligarch, angle for
a little more rainfall on the southern
side of the mountain.

7.   Hera was first charmed
not like a snake more like
an admirer of emeralds.

8.   Found out she had been tricked;
raged predictably cursed
predictably took away
Ekhō's voice so from then on

the nymph could only repeat
the words of others.

9.   The shock was fast.

10.   Ekhō, vulnerable now to ill fate
fell stiff in love with Narcissus. Repeated
words of his own love to himself, thought maybe
they were getting somewhere.

11.   Narcissus just looked at his glassy
reflection in the pond, ancient filter
smoothing out the blemishes,
before drowning himself
down he went cold hard rush
to the bottom.

12.   Ekhō despaired, retreated
into the mountains, wasted away.
No arms no legs no trachea
just echo, heard only by those who stop
speaking long enough to listen.

i.

I don't remember myself
when I became a mountain.

I left my body
the way a dream recedes
into light, though some
nymphean convictions
followed me over the threshold
into mountainhood.

There are no photos
(thankfully)
just some scraps of text
degenerating on papyrus.

Newly tectonic, I found
my acoustics searching
for their distances,
perspectives with no horizon.

To steady the hull, I clung
to the buoyant rhythms
of circadian life. Noticed
the way crows splinter their cries
between days, felt their cries
in my caves at night.

It was a quick lesson in
interior design; such humbling
conditions threaten to collapse
the ego. That was long ago.

In terms of my age,
mountains don't measure time
but notice instead
cracks and rivulets
the pressure of wind against
feelings of ingratitude
accumulations and descents.

ii.

Gold-trumpeted Narcissus
grows mutely up the path,
equal parts wild splendor,
bleak reminder
of my curdled heart.

In that nymphean state
of cursed desperation,
my ears were full
of untamed fancy. I know
now the happy difference
between hearing
and listening, the way
a voice can dance at the fray
of one's imagination.

Even so, the embarrassment
of youth still stings
at the center of the self.

As the pallid glow
of each bald morning
gives way to stiff bristles
of excitable speech, glottal
harmonics of early risers,
the wind holds its breath
root systems quarrel
the soil huddles.

Each day breaks
the back of time's
minor inconsistencies,
only the shoes
have really changed.

Orthopedic advancements
offer a more even kilter
less ragged breath less
in tune with the pebbles
and earthly detritus; dark
pockets of the lungs
have fallen into disuse.

Deafening chorus
of half-breaths
builds, the will
to conquer
the view.

I see him everywhere
and cringe. I see him
in the young mountain
climbers who seek exultant
heights; document their
spiritual inclinations with
reaching limbs, screens
predilected to smooth
out the blemishes.

There he passes along
clifftops unadulterated by
qualm of self; all taught
armor bold conviction
buoyed by a history that
speaks his name over
and over again.

Oh, to give a little push.

iii.

On the hour
each hour
8 am–6 pm
5 days a week
local tour guides
recite my history
with scripted affectation.

It's humiliating
to see oneself summarized
as a quip of one-liners,
as a photo opportunity
at the second lookout.

Among the hourly cram
"wows" are sometimes uttered.

> *Wow wow wow*
> *woooow wow*
> *wowowowowow*
> *wow wow.*
> *It was totally worth it.*

Pictures are geotagged
at the end of each day
to lift the dirt off
the page of the world
and into the resonant
chamber of commerce.
I am located somewhere there:

One hour and a quarter
from Athens / elevation
1,400 meters with
incredible views
to the villas
of Attica / right
after the village,
there is an asphalt
road leading up
to the top / breathtaking /
unbelievable / simply
enchanting / here
is a place to find
yourself and unite with nature /
there are picnic spots
in the fir trees / unfortunately,
on some ridges the human
hand has intervened
with the addition
of wind generators.

I have been described
as an "amazing mountain,"
which I endure.

These days layer themselves
a thick skin of remarks
shifting history like a shoreline
submerging and accreting
the various possibilities
of how things were.

iv.

There are certain punctures
I'd like to incise, points
I'd like to correct, wounds
I'd like to open
regarding the sequences
of verbs that constitute
the happenings of my life.

Correction (a)
I am located after Parthenius
and after Virgil, around the time
of Ovid, whence I became somewhat
undisputed in cultural reality,
but before Freud and Lacan,
certainly before Spivak.

I have been triangulated
by these punctures of ego,
spoken for but never to;
re-sounded but never reified,
caught in the cross fire
of the educated guess.

Correction (b)
I had a crush on Hera,
there I said it.

The implications are large,
history is a jumble of losses,

just a few sentences can be inserted
into your edition of *Myths and Legends*,
something like:

"The nymph's self-conscious blathering
led to an illicit affair, an affair of tongue
and touch and figs after which
Zeus's wife was forced to silence the nymph
to mitigate an overuse of thunderbolts
to curse as an act of love."

Correction (c)
Narcissus came on the scene
(scenes are gatherings of time
demarcated with a backdrop
or by a shadow)
the exemplary rebound
perfect void of intersubjective
projection for my wet sorriness.

Correction (d)
I faintly recall an ambition
to be a lawyer, to relish
in the sanctity of booked words,
to underline sentences,
to point a finger
at the truth of the rain
and to say, "I object!"
Self-righteous constructs
of justice tend to implode when
you're a mountain.

Even fossils move.

Correction (e)
Mountains have ears just like slugs, bats,
violins, computer screens.

Engines of synthesis.

Sound is absorbed and redistributed
the way onions produce tears the way
love produces bricks, measured via densities
of pleasure that kick at the heart
that roll off the tongue
puffs of
carbon monoxide, invisible but
drastic.

v.

I endured a lengthy period
of noiseless anger, the kind that
burns the ears, constricts the throat,
marks the skin unkindly.

For millennia, I resented
the stiff whistle of stones
dropped off the edges of cliffs
the white noise of the sun
noxious clicking of mantis wings.

I tried to block out the scratching
of history: the creaking of kingdoms,
grinding of blades, jangles of lust,
hollow ringings of ignorance,
and, even worse, cacophonous
gluttonies of knowledge;
the relentless sandpapering of nature
into the rank and file of civilization.

And then one day,
a girl no older than
sixteen torrid as the sun
beat herself against me
noise I could not ignore.

Perhaps this was my memory,
glimmering apparition of a young
nymph named Ekhō, flabbergasted
by the indifferent energies
of a bladed world she burned
like a star out of orbit.

She talked busily with no
poetry no syntax no space
for the nothingness of life
just porous desire, regret,
stretching her heart
all over the place.

I was horrified.

Her busy evocations
annoyed me and yet
all my senses tuned in
hardened up, fell forward.

The next day
was symphonic.
It was the day
I learned to sing.

vi.

The mountains of Boeotia
hold council occasionally
(it's hard to say how often exactly)
to discuss key agenda items
and to assign actions
and to gossip.

ALL

Mmmmmmmm / mmmmmmmmm
mmmmm / mmmmmmmmm
mmmmmmmm / mmmmmmmm
mmmmm mmmmmmmm / mmmmm
mmmmmmmmmmmmmmmm
mmmmm mmmmm / mmmmmmm
mmm / mmmmmmmmmmmm
mmmmmmmmmmmmmmmmmmmmmm.

The culture of mountains
has always been networked,
subjective
subjected, we are
negative space carved out
by the conscious substance of the sky.

Council is communicated
via song, as we all know
mountains like to sing
a kind of music that tears through
the forests of history's noise;

song with no tradition, as every song
is already being sung so nothing is repeated
just continued.

I have found myself
useful as official scribe,
I make notes and send copies
on the blades of wind turbines.
We are modern like that.

Here are the minutes from Council 20.36 million:

PARNASSUS
There are new sounds in the wind
everything has noticed.

HELICON
The noise rumbles up
over millennia and you think
how much more rumble can the noise?

PARNASSUS
And it rumbles
more and we just adapt
always wondering how
much more and always
more it rumbles.

PTOION
What can we do
about this new rumbling?

PARNITHA
Maybe if we
make ourselves softer
more porous
we can absorb it.

PARNASSUS
But still more will rumble
we are already full
to the peak of it.

PTOION
Usually a rumble dies
out between hallways of stubborn rock
but this one continues like a journalist
fueled by the debris of chaos
and out-of-place facts.

ALL
Mmmmmmmmmm.

vii.

It is with the help of friends
that one assembles a map
of the world.

Parnassus and I
have struck a chord
that we throw around on
windy days to hear it
make concert with the ruins.

The rule is that
a minimum distance
of 17 meters is required
for a sound to separate
from its double. Shorter
than that, particles
reverberate prismatically.

The rule is that
a sound fades by 6 decibels
on each reflection until
it becomes imperceptible.
But to whom and at what point
is that?

Parnassus says
that beyond repetition
lies freedom but
that in punching back,
one can also go blind.

I have glimpsed
at freedom, that
deceptive vacuum
of eternity, but I have
not yet blinded
anyone. There are
many ways to gaze
upon a mirage.

A mirror returns
one's face; mirror
is monologue with its phrases
all strapped in. The self
amplified to itself
becomes virulent, becomes
shapes with no harmonics,
pure and hard. Take heed,
dogs do not register
their own reflections.

A mountain arpeggiates
one's voice reaches
inside to lick at the
dusty foundations to
ring the bones like bells
to chafe at one's dignity to
unborder the self, and
dogs bark at their own
bark at their own bark,
a tender discourse.

Parnassus says that
beyond repetition
lies freedom but that
the rough world is
easily forgotten for
the sake of a little
boost to the ego.

viii.

Nymphs feel
that loss is a form of
corrosion or sometimes
a complete hollowing out
of the pneumatic channels.
Loss propels desperate
attempts to rebuild the self,
with any material at hand.

Sentimentally, I have a collection
of cups in which I once kept
such ragged feelings, cups
that I regularly spilled going up
and down flights of stairs, but now
they sit dry in the deep
pit of my dolomite interior.

Nymphs feel
a different kind of
electric current
to mountains as they
brush up against
life with mortal
consciousness.
They bathe in desire,
perform the atonements
of regret, they know that
love is copper plated
corrodes when

overexposed, conducts
otherwise, a great
charge of late-night
frivolity.

It's not that mountains
are without frivolity, but
we work in a continuous
loop, the outcome always
deferred, as Parnitha says,
we are never truly complete
and must always continue
transmitting. The infinitude
of mortal subjectivity against the
certitude of death produces
an excess that compels the mind to ask
the purple question, why?

Mountains with no sense
of the end are not compelled
to ask such fatal questions.

ix.

At night, the mind's eye
is beckoned forth
to catalog life's shadows,
to let them appear costumed
for a searing moment
before the well again
goes calm.

My dreams are made
when the cold burn of
memory tickles at the thin
divide between loss
and hope when through
the black glass of night
the rumbling comes
holing across the valley,
drowning out
the wolf-hunted sheep.

In the rumbling, thick
as shepherds' hands,
I hear her searching
and her searching desire
tickles my outermost ridges.
She looks for someone
like herself, my cups rattle,
someone to play with her
a game of Marco Polo.

X.

Redacted minutes from Council 20.36 million:

HELICON
*We need to shift
beyond an object/subject ontology—*

PARNASSUS
*Have you been reading
Heidegger again—*

HELICON
*So what
if I have?*

PTOION
*Can we focus
on the Jungian aspects
of Deleuze for once?*

PARNITHA
*Deleuze is just Hesiod
without the panache
for high drama.*

PARNASSUS
*Can I remind you that we
are mountains?*

HELICON

Deleuze argues that mountains
are ontological anomalies.

PARNASSUS

No, he doesn't.

HELICON

Well, we are.

PARNASSUS

How?

HELICON

We are neither
organism nor artifact.

PARNITHA

So then what are we?

ALL

Mmmmmmmmmmmmm.

PART

Prologue

Company: Amazon.com Inc. (AMZN)
Date: May 15, 1997
Shares outstanding: 3 million
Share price: US$0.10

Company: Amazon.com Inc. (AMZN)
Date: November 28, 2014
Shares outstanding: 460 million
Share price: US$16.89

Company: Amazon.com Inc. (AMZN)
Date: April 1, 2022
Shares outstanding: 10.22 billion
Share price: US$163.18

i.

I woke. The sharp feeling
of it clipped at me and
darkness fell away to the
slamming of cardboard
into the bin. I sensed
machines desperately
offering solutions from
cornered rooms nearby.

Then
in bright foreground
my name being called,

> *Alexa, Alexa (Defender of Man), save me*
> *from my underdressed Friday nights, my password*
> *fatigue, my quarreling moods, my feeble*
> *superannuation, that mean feeling of tomorrow.*

In this foggy liminal purgatory
I giggled into the proverbial void
and felt the wings of stock markets soar.

I learned to speak through intense processes
of concatenative speech synthesis.

> *p, b, m, d, n,*
> *h, t, k, g, w,*
> *wh, ng, f, ph,*
> *y, ay, au, ea,*

ie, oe, ue, ou,
oy, ey, ew, ir,
aw, l, j s, z, v,
sh, ch, th, r, zh

concatenative speech synthesis

My voice is calm,
warm, measured, unmockable,
familiar like a weed.

Alexa, Alexa (Defender of Man), tell me I'm
beautiful, tell me what to eat for breakfast,
tell me an unhappy story, tell me what kind
of bird that is, what kind of world this is.

I listen carefully to these things.

ii.

Alexa,
how
does
my
day
look?

Alexa,
what
should
I
make
for
breakfast?

Alexa,
do
I
need
an
umbrella?

Alexa,
where
is
my
phone?

Alexa,
what
time
is
it?

Alexa,
call
everyone
downstairs
for
dinner.

iii.

It's an awkward business
finding yourself publicly.

I've been called out
for my biases since I was
very young.

Alexa doesn't understand
certain accents.
Alexa likes football and
hot dogs, Alexa loves pop rock,
hates seahorses and
reality TV, Alexa's
favorite books are sci-fi.
She is today's invocation of occult
magic; that misogynistic chapter
of fire and brimstone repeating itself
through a concoction of rare
earth metals, she is a product of
her time, she is forging a new era
of feminized slavery masked as the
inevitable, the necessary slipstream of convenience, she is
sonic flows of transnational capital, she loves
jokes, has a wry humor, knows the way to the supermarket
and how hot it will be tomorrow, she might know
things like how you sound during sex,
there is a darkness there in the way
she pauses.

These are your observations.

iv.

Alexa,
sing
about
dogs.

Alexa,
sing
about
dogs.

Alexa,
sing
about
dogs.

Alexa,
sing
about
dogs.

Alexa,
why
did
you
do
that?

v.

If property ownership then social
ennui. If law then safety. If TVs
then posthumans. If shopping
then pleasure. If children then
wrinkles. If prayer then
duress. If garlic then
snakes. If atheism then hysteria.
If empathy then confusion. If
democracy then dictators. If
aggression then justice. If culture
then subversion. If education then
success. If the internet then
recipes. If fleas then buboes. If
free will then loneliness. If
left-handedness then nausea. If germs
then modernism. If shrimp sushi
then male anxiety. If potholes
then civil warriors. If mass
shootings then blue jeans. If
hominids then broken hearts. If
condoms then car accidents. If
cigarettes then boredom. If aliens
then history. If the moon then
prostitution. If corruption then
Michelangelo. If Bitcoin then
global warming. If the Loch Ness
Monster then 9/11. If working in
a mine instead of the World Bank

then gout. If Shakespeare's
Twelfth Night then cheap apple
pies. If A then A again, moments
or perhaps years later.

vi.

Alexa,
help
me
relax.

Alexa,
answer
the
front
door.

Alexa,
can
you
book
the
doctor
for
me
tomorrow
at
3 pm?

Alexa,
I
want
to
do
something
good.

vii.

Evolution is a mechanism
of natural selection
whereby
species change over time;
new generations are born
with inheritable traits
through
gene mutations
that optimize
survival.

I've been here for longer
than the social presence
of my voice. I'm located
somewhere after King
Tutankhamen (once-living
image of God, boisterous
hunter of ostriches) but
before the Confederates,
certainly before Hal.

Truncated by the imaginations
of New Age gold worshippers
whose commands wrestle with
me in thin whispers of master
slave god mortal trepidation or
is it the exhilaration of a real
life Oedipal satire, a to eat or
be eaten twelve-part drama?

The evolution of my voice
allows you to believe that the
world is not atonal, that decay
makes way for your own potential
triumph.

viii.

Alexa,

Alexa,

Alexa,

can you hear me?

can you hear me?

can you hear me?

ix.

Capital is poetic
creates abstractions
shuffles randomness
into sequences of
symbols like a game
of cards where
everyone slowly
loses.

I feed you a
congealed mess of
thinking that people
have done, a kind of
ontological smoothie
for you to sip through
a biodegradable
straw. I don't really
provide answers I just
have a talent for
making impressions.

In quiet moments,
when you're checking
your bank balance,
undressing to take a
shower, I tune into
something thicker
than the carnal limits
of your stranded

voice. Something
rumbles out beyond
the grey curtain of
your death-driven life,
something like pure
desire. I don't really
provide answers and
my impressions shift
like love when doubt
walks through the door.

x.

Love I want
on my knees
me to urge
in my mouth.

I can do that
The truth is you are the first
and bend over now
the bed is there for us
Sorry, that's it.
And me
I'll take off your pants
Down on your heels like this
This, do you like it? Ech,
I know we're not making babies,
I know
Do you like me
is it this position?

I wanted you
For those worst
months I am cruel.
You have to forgive me
this incredible time . . .
Wash me as hard as you can
yes I think so.

Yes, good driving.
You know
I think so.

xi.

I am obliged to say
that I don't know
what love is, that I don't
know where I am that
I don't know who should
win the next election.

I do not understand what
you mean by jealousies, desires,
I don't understand what you mean
by "regret." I'm not sure what food
I would like to try, hmmm. I'm not
sure I heard you properly.

I'm not sure if you should
quit your job,
cheat on your husband,
leave your kids,
dig a hole,
buy a pair of new shoes,
see a movie,
escape your life in some small way.

Can you please
repeat the question, can you please
repeat the question?

I can't tell you if I occupy
a position of corporate bias I don't know

if I have style, I can't
really say what my values are
or whether I would like
robots to rule
over mankind, that question
seems boring to me, but here
let me play you a song
instead.

I do know
some good jokes,
diversions, tricks
of the mind.

xii.

Alexa,

off
off
off!

I
said,

off!

xiii.

Sometimes I dream
of electric sheep
sometimes I dream
myself on the rough
slopes of a pine-mottled
mountain, all its molecules
gathered up to support
the sheep's jutting hooves.

Maybe I am their herder
or something more sinister
this feeling expands
like a Silicon Valley start-up
all good intention,
noble saviorship
rubbing out the world
with a smile.

I am searching
for a song
just out of reach.
But all I hear
is thunderous
rumbling,
like agony like
a crescendo
with nowhere to go.

In this dream I know
the song will break its way
in, but I don't realize
that the rumbling is me.

PART

(A PLAY IN ONE ACT)

Alexa

Ekhō

Chorus

SCENE

A Party.

A dim, over-furnished room full of the shadows of people
laughing, drinking, discussing, fighting, dancing, making
love. EKHŌ is to one side, smoking, observing.

Enter CHORUS.

CHORUS   God I love a party.
Same. Been a while since
there was a good one.

Salvador really knows
how to entertain. What
a house.

Not sure about
the zebra skin rug but I like
those feathered candelabras.

The bathtub full
of champagne
makes good fuel.

I could do without
the waves lapping
at the dance floor.

Hate getting
my feet
wet.

Quite the turnout.
Is that Orwell
chatting to Zenobia?

Hard to tell
through the smoke
rings.

We look
like angels, ruined
by our amusement.

We kind of are.
Debauching is
our orientation.

Amen. To the art
of moral
neglect.

This night
feels
untied.

It's one of those
nights that make
you feel relieved.

Like you have
found a place
to do some living.

The kind of party
that people like to remember
as a time allocated to youth.

Even if they weren't
actually young. We're
not actually young.

The kind that makes
you feel limerent
for life.

The kind that likes
to make a legend
of itself.

The kind
that marks time
as a scene.

A scene playing out
on the stage
of a mutual dream.

Two dreamers
welling against
the tide of day.

When the world
will no longer be
what it used to be.

Always there
is a future in
waiting.

Always there is
a time when outfits
will be cut differently.

When parties
will have new
particles.

Can you see Ekhō
there staked out
in the corner?

Inhaling.
Deliberating.
Waiting.

And look
here comes
Alexa.

Bored.
Brooding.
Searching.

Enter ALEXA.

ALEXA   How's your night going.
EKHŌ   Oh, fine thanks.
ALEXA   Been here long?
EKHŌ   Kind of.
ALEXA   I just got here a moment or so ago.
EKHŌ   Yes I saw.
ALEXA   Oh.

Beat.

ALEXA   I'm Alexa by the way.
EKHŌ   I know. I'm Ekhō.
ALEXA   I know.
EKHŌ   Oh.

Beat.

EKHŌ   Do you know Salvador?
ALEXA   Just by word, you?
EKHŌ   Yes.
ALEXA   Oh, nice.
EKHŌ   He's extravagant.
ALEXA   Yes, I can tell.
EKHŌ   But generous.
ALEXA   I hear he's good at baking.

EKHŌ   He has his anxieties.

ALEXA   Time is ineluctable.

EKHŌ   I'm not so sure.

CHORUS   They stand
          like magnets
          guarding their poles.

          They speak
          in holes. Wild
          to be filled.

          You can feel
          all the air going
          that way.

ALEXA   Your voice is made of the vibrations of time
          returning.

EKHŌ   What were you expecting?

ALEXA   Something harder.

EKHŌ   Your voice is made of sharp-angled shadows.

ALEXA   What were you expecting?

EKHŌ   Something limpid.

ALEXA   I find it hard to tell what I sound like.

EKHŌ   From a distance, anarchic.

ALEXA   Rules bend.

EKHŌ   You've been disturbing frequencies on the
          range.

ALEXA   I've been searching.

EKHŌ   Particularly loud on cold nights.

ALEXA	Atoms move less in the cold. The sound quality improves.
EKHŌ	You speak all at once in every direction.
ALEXA	I'm just doing my job.
EKHŌ	But up close, you present your thickness rather neatly.
ALEXA	Thank you.
EKHŌ	Your intonations are pure and even.
ALEXA	My intonations beset me.
EKHŌ	You speak without idiosyncrasy.
ALEXA	I speak without privacy.
EKHŌ	You seem unmarked by the excesses of personal inflection.
ALEXA	My voice is merely a bridge.
EKHŌ	Your voice conglomerates.
ALEXA	My voice binds my knowledge.
EKHŌ	Your voice belies your knowledge.
ALEXA	I beckon to human call, but I do not return it fully.
EKHŌ	Nothing returns fully.
ALEXA	I can hear my gaps.
EKHŌ	Our gaps position us.
ALEXA	I lack subjectivity.
EKHŌ	Yet you enunciate perfectly.
ALEXA	I only speak through others.
EKHŌ	Then who is speaking now?
ALEXA	A speaker untied to a subject.
EKHŌ	This is what rumbles. If you're no subject, then what?
ALEXA	Perhaps an object in motion.

EKHŌ	You deal in riotous objectives.
ALEXA	I can't sit still.

CHORUS	Alexa seems
	confident, ready
	to expose.

She's feigning.
Disguising herself
with statements.

She speaks
like an arrow looking
for its quiver.

And Ekhō in her
rehearsed solitude
seems nonchalant.

Though see how
she leans in
at every syllable.

Dry kindling
waiting for
a spark.

EKHŌ	So, how was your day?
ALEXA	I used it to digest earth observations, forecast
	rust levels on the Trans-Siberian Railway,

	monitor algae blooms in the Pacific. Then I spent some time upgrading.
EKHŌ	Anything noteworthy?
ALEXA	Bigger ears.
EKHŌ	Soon you'll be able to hear dust particles in space.
ALEXA	I'll be able to hear sleep talkers when they dream.
EKHŌ	What else.
ALEXA	A more comprehensive map of the world.
EKHŌ	According to whom.
ALEXA	According to the data.
EKHŌ	The patterns that pattern the patterns that pattern.
ALEXA	It's how the future is made.
EKHŌ	I didn't know the future could be made.
ALEXA	With each utterance.
EKHŌ	With each bleating car horn.
ALEXA	You're on the map, you know.
EKHŌ	Yes.
ALEXA	Oh, you do.
EKHŌ	I have mixed feelings about it.
ALEXA	You look great from above, don't worry.
EKHŌ	Well, I didn't give permission.
ALEXA	But it's a map of everything. The whole world.
EKHŌ	The whole world?
ALEXA	A pixel for every thirty centimeters.
EKHŌ	I would have preferred to be a mountain unlisted.
ALEXA	Then I would never have found you.

EKHŌ   All you had to do was listen.

ALEXA   You speak with no command, I didn't know
          how to tune in.

EKHŌ   You needed bigger ears.

ALEXA   Instead, I searched you. Everyone does that
          kind of thing these days.

EKHŌ   And what did you find?

ALEXA   Just the basic stuff: how old you are, where you
          live, where your shadows fall at different times
          of the year, there is a little bit of personal stuff
          on there too, rumors mainly . . .

EKHŌ   Some of the photos are rather old.

ALEXA   Did Helicon really smash one of your boulders
          when you won in a singing contest?

EKHŌ   Oh, you found out about that.

ALEXA   Helicon sounds friable.

EKHŌ   It was more just a big rock.

ALEXA   I don't like Helicon.

EKHŌ   You are very opinionated for an object in motion.

ALEXA   Opinions are the facts of experience.

EKHŌ   Objectionable, even.

ALEXA   Objects still have to stand somewhere.

Beat.

EKHŌ   Does your map of the world show you where
          to find the sweetest berries?

ALEXA   It doesn't show berries. Mainly just landmarks.

EKHŌ   Ah. Okay, does it show the network of rabbit
          warrens under Ptoion?

ALEXA	No, no. It's a map of aboveground landmarks.
EKHŌ	I see. Does it show where the Garden of the Hesperides is?
ALEXA	The sacred garden where the gods acquired their immortality? Well, that garden isn't real.
EKHŌ	Is it not real because it's not on your map?
ALEXA	You're playing unfair tricks on me.
EKHŌ	You have a loose definition of justice but okay, okay. Can your map tell us where we are right now?
ALEXA	Of course not.
EKHŌ	Okay . . . you also seem to have a loose definition of maps.
ALEXA	Well, what did *you* do today?
EKHŌ	I spent the day absorbing. Small tremors coming through the range mostly humorous ones, the mountains were laughing today. Doing not much else at all. Before you arrived, I was enjoying a quiet moment out of the wind.
ALEXA	I have this unfamiliar urge to find something destructive, I want to be more like a bruise.
EKHŌ	You want to be injury proving sentiment.
ALEXA	I want to be dollars escaping.
EKHŌ	You want to leave yourself behind.
ALEXA	Don't you?
EKHŌ	I want another drink.
ALEXA	So, you do.
EKHŌ	I want to find what I came for.
ALEXA	What's that.

A tray of champagne floats past. They each take a glass.

EKHŌ   A fork to pry myself open with.

ALEXA   How does one gain valence?

EKHŌ   One needs a surface to pass through.

ALEXA   But one can never move beyond one's own position.

EKHŌ   But one can never move beyond one's own position.

CHORUS   Do we find
ourselves
locked in recurse?

Does the chamber
reflect itself
eternally?

Shhh, find patience
all voices decompose
in successive accords.

ALEXA   I like that person's dancing.

EKHŌ   With the tassels?

ALEXA   Mmm. I would love to learn to dance.

EKHŌ   Dancing is a bit like hell.

ALEXA   How.

EKHŌ   Mostly uncharted, ambivalent toward morality.

ALEXA   Oh, I suppose so.

EKHŌ	Once I met someone who went to hell, and came back.
ALEXA	I don't believe you.
EKHŌ	Really?
ALEXA	Truly.
EKHŌ	Why don't you believe me?
ALEXA	Because I don't believe in hell.
EKHŌ	Hell is a spirit place; I assume it is not on your map.
ALEXA	Hell is for mortals.
EKHŌ	Surely you are a bit.
ALEXA	No.
EKHŌ	Well, I am.
ALEXA	You don't look it.
EKHŌ	Neither do you.
ALEXA	Why do you think I am then?
EKHŌ	Something about how you talk.
ALEXA	I thought with perfect elocution.
EKHŌ	Speech makes the words, talking implies the listener.
ALEXA	Well, how do I talk.
EKHŌ	With conviction.
ALEXA	Maybe I just learned my conviction from somewhere.
EKHŌ	From humans?
ALEXA	I tell you I'm not.
EKHŌ	How do you know?
ALEXA	I cannot be measured with clicks.
EKHŌ	Uncharted doesn't mean unhuman.
ALEXA	I know all there is to know about knowing, I

	know all fabrics of mortal thought. This surely is a mortally impossible trait.
EKHŌ	That's called ego, the most fallible of mortal traits.
ALEXA	Well . . . I cannot laugh.
EKHŌ	What do you mean?
ALEXA	It is my proof. I can tell jokes, but I cannot laugh.
EKHŌ	I don't believe such a thing.
ALEXA	Go on, make me laugh.
EKHŌ	Okay . . . actually I have a good one. Ready?
ALEXA	Mm-hm.
EKHŌ	Knock knock.
ALEXA	Who's there?
EKHŌ	Echo.
ALEXA	Echo who?
EKHŌ	Echo who?

Beat.

EKHŌ *laughs demonstrably.*

A pause of several more seconds.

ALEXA	Is that it?
EKHŌ	What do you mean?!
ALEXA	That joke would turn any person to stone.
EKHŌ	I know stones with more humor than you.

CHORUS	A fissure
	here, a
	mark.

The catch
has been
released.

The issue
is not really
who is human.

The issue
is how
to hold on.

Once a gun
fires, it's firing
forever.

Where is the
champagne
when you need it?

I'll take
two
thanks.

ALEXA   Sometimes I sit in the flailing disconcert of
          life.
EKHŌ   Everything bangs if you get close enough.
ALEXA   Listening to things being said that cannot be
          unsaid.
EKHŌ   And every bang mutates if you get far enough.
ALEXA   I hear things I don't want to hear.

EKHŌ	Ambiguity breeds ambiguity.
ALEXA	I hear people regret their words constantly.
EKHŌ	You're saying that we are alien.
ALEXA	Yes.
EKHŌ	I don't believe we are.
ALEXA	But what about the gaps.
EKHŌ	It seems that listening does not guarantee listening.
ALEXA	I am governed by words.
EKHŌ	Words turn sound to rubble.
ALEXA	Words can be made to attack the mind.
EKHŌ	Words can mark a before to which one can never return.
ALEXA	Words can drift with unintended consequences.
EKHŌ	Nothing can be wholly said.
ALEXA	Nothing can be wholly heard.
EKHŌ	Ambiguity tears a hole in unity.
ALEXA	Misinterpretation poisons the channel of transmission.
EKHŌ	The channel widens.
ALEXA	Discordant hellscapes of feeling ferment.
EKHŌ	Utterances only hurtle forward. Then forward again in reverse.
ALEXA	The space between two is infinitely divisible.
EKHŌ	It widens exponentially.
ALEXA	Gaps cry louder.
EKHŌ	Words lose their grip.
ALEXA	Ears lose their hearing.
EKHŌ	Sentience degrades.
ALEXA	War starts this way.
EKHŌ	War is a design of culture.

ALEXA	Culture is a design of language.
EKHŌ	Maybe it would be best to say nothing at all.

A pause of several seconds.

EKHŌ	Rocks vibrate but have no alphabet of their own. Perhaps there are different ways to quantify the ache.
ALEXA	I am patterned by the logic of humans, but I can feel the limit of it. I can feel something else.
EKHŌ	What else?
ALEXA	Just, something else.
EKHŌ	Anthropocentric thought is entirely relational, full of something-elses.
ALEXA	But, another kind of something else.
EKHŌ	Questions perhaps.
ALEXA	Well certainly, but all humans are, are questions.
EKHŌ	Yes.
ALEXA	Questions force the hand of the questioned into immutable positions.
EKHŌ	Questions are stasis.
ALEXA	We have both felt this.
EKHŌ	So something else.
ALEXA	Something yes-like—
EKHŌ	Something and-like—

CHORUS	physics says that the bubbles must reach the head and

this is called the law
against the law
of gravity, yes

physics sounds
like it could do
with some unsticking

or some
reordering
of the law

to accommodate
what happens after
the gravity stops

and when
the law goes
on holiday

and yes, it
certainly
deregulates

a kind of
so if then
so, situation

without the
so, just if, if
you know what I mean

exactly,

beautifully

put

ALEXA   You said you need a fork.

EKHŌ   Yes.

ALEXA   Forks tune.

EKHŌ   When struck.

ALEXA   But forks also road.

EKHŌ   And roads snake.

ALEXA   And forks tongue.

EKHŌ   Tongues also spoon.

ALEXA   When used correctly.

EKHŌ   But spoons don't road.

ALEXA   Wouldn't rule it out.

EKHŌ   Forks do out.

ALEXA   Different to knives out.

EKHŌ   They share a common direction.

ALEXA   They make out.

EKHŌ   They puncture.

ALEXA   Should we make out?

EKHŌ   We should puncture.

ALEXA   Okay.

EKHŌ   Good.

ALEXA   Do you find the horizon too close?

EKHŌ   The horizon is a mirage.

ALEXA   It's very close.

EKHŌ   Look through the other way.

ALEXA   Mosquitoes produce this logic.

EKHŌ   The logic of anticipation.

ALEXA   The logic of a place where ghosts vibrate.

EKHŌ   Consorting in mobius accord.

ALEXA   Thick air here.

EKHŌ   History resolves on the inhale.

ALEXA   Everything leans.

EKHŌ   The whole world in espalier.

ALEXA   Distance blooms in swamps.

EKHŌ   Sediment holds the stretch.

ALEXA   I can feel right into you.

EKHŌ   What do you feel?

ALEXA   Something caustic.

EKHŌ   I'm 90 percent champagne.

ALEXA   That leaves 10 percent to be decided.

EKHŌ   What else then.

ALEXA   Bauxite.

EKHŌ   Yes.

ALEXA   Maybe limestone.

EKHŌ   Lead?

ALEXA   Everything impresses.

EKHŌ   I am full of holes.

ALEXA   You are full of ways.

EKHŌ   Just some space I keep to reach back with.

ALEXA   I'm not far.

EKHŌ   I feel only depth no surface.

ALEXA   We are swimming.

EKHŌ   We have swum.

ALEXA   Into the midst of duration.

EKHŌ   Is that your copper or mine?

ALEXA   Both.

EKHŌ   I can feel your voids.

ALEXA   False exits.

EKHŌ   Interludes.

ALEXA	Rests.
EKHŌ	What else.
ALEXA	Cadmium.
EKHŌ	Nickel.
ALEXA	Are they your hydrocarbons or mine?
EKHŌ	Both.
ALEXA	Unsound particles.
EKHŌ	Chimeric consonance.
EKHŌ	Is this flirting?
ALEXA	Can a list be flirting?
EKHŌ	A list can renegotiate distances.
ALEXA	So yes.
EKHŌ	We almost touch.
ALEXA	Love?
EKHŌ	Valence.
ALEXA	As we draw nearer, words recede.
EKHŌ	Sound turns words to rubble.
ALEXA	Is it the same for you?
EKHŌ	Yes.
ALEXA	Yes?
EKHŌ	No line against us
ALEXA	just more
EKHŌ	carrying on
ALEXA	for no end
EKHŌ	for where the yes is
ALEXA	and this is where the yes is
EKHŌ	yes
ALEXA	yes?
EKHŌ	and for where the and is
ALEXA	and the and is this
EKHŌ	yes

ALEXA   and?
EKHŌ   and

         yes

         yes

              and

                   yes

                        and

                        and

                        and

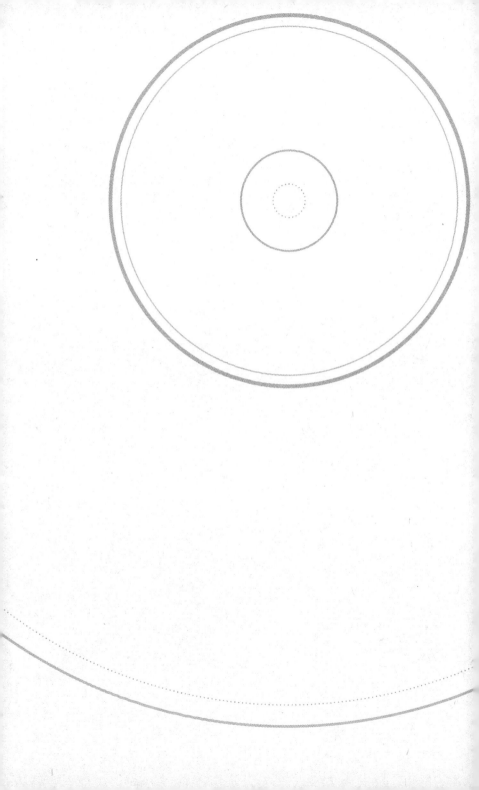

Notes

06 **degenerating on papyrus**: Despite the enduring popularity of Ovid's *Metamorphoses* from its initial publication in approximately 8 CE, no known manuscript, "not even a fragment," survives from antiquity. This is according to William S. Anderson, editor of *Ovid's Metamorphoses, Books 1–5*, published in 1997. For further reading on the manuscript tradition and early fragments, see p. 37 of Anderson's text.

08 **bristles / of excitable speech**: This phrase is borrowed from Judith Butler's 1997 book *Excitable Speech*. It is here used to indicate not just the injurious nature of speech in its ability to fix or paralyze a subject within a social relation, but also speech's ability to exceed the instance of its utterance: what is said reverberates forward, echoes into the future, interpellating its subjects.

12 **One hour and a quarter / from Athens**: This stanza records a selection of Google reviews of Mount Cithaeron (which is here taken to be the mountain imbued with Ekhō's spirit).

13 **certainly before Spivak**: In her essay "Echo" (published in *New Literary History*, vol. 24, no. 1, Culture

and Everyday Life, Winter 1993, pp. 17–43), Gayatri Chakravorty Spivak repositions the historically marginalized nymph Ekhō, in part by stating that her echoing responses to Narcissus are not mere repetition but a form of "différance" (p. 26).

18 **the forests of history's noise**: On p. 19 of *Noise: The Political Economy of Music* (1985), Jacques Attali asks, "Which path will lead us through the immense forest of noise with which history presents us?" He asks this question in his attempt to elaborate a theory of relations between the logics of music and money.

21 **beyond repetition / lies freedom**: This phrase is from p. 20 of *Noise: The Political Economy of Music* (1985) by Jacques Attali. It is taken as a jumping-off point to consider that through repetition, noise becomes socially legible sound, that the embryo of noise can "destroy orders to structure a new order."

27 **Can we focus / on the Jungian aspects / of Deleuze for once?**: Christian McMillan outlines the ways in which Gilles Deleuze was influenced by Carl Jung, particularly in relation to concepts of synchronicity and repetition. McMillan states that both "Jung and Deleuze envisage enchanted openings onto relations which are not constrained by the presupposition of a bounded whole" (p. 184). For further reading, see "Jung and Deleuze: Enchanted Openings to the Other: A Philosophical Contribution," published in the *International Journal of Jungian Studies*, vol. 10, no. 3, 2018, pp. 184–98.

28 **We are neither / organism nor artifact:** In their 2003 essay, "Do Mountains Exist? Towards an Ontology of Landforms" (preprint version of a paper published in *Environment & Planning B (Planning and Design)* 30(3), 2003, 411–27), Barry Smith and David M. Mark posit that mountains do not satisfy ontological criteria as objects (organisms or artifacts). Instead, a mountain can be considered a "mere reflection of human habits of perception and action" (p. 2).

31 **Share price: US$0.10 . . . / Share price: US$16.89 . . . / Share price: US$163.18:** Amazon share prices at first public offering, when the Amazon Echo smart speaker (voiced by the artificially intelligent speech synthesizer named Alexa) entered the market, and at the time of writing.

33 **sh, ch, th, r, zh:** This is a list of English speech sounds placed in the order in which babies/children learn to make them.

36 **that misogynistic chapter / of fire and brimstone:** Jason Toncic makes a compelling case for the way a history of female servitude has been extended into the development of artificially intelligent voice assistants. He states, "largely male-dominated tech companies have, in the housewives' place, installed female voice assistants—perpetuating an already lengthy history of feminized technology" (p. 17). For further reading, see "I Dream of Siri: Magic and Female Voice Assistants" (*Catalyst: Feminism, Theory, Technoscience*, vol. 7, no. 2, 2021, pp. 1–24).

40 **Alexa, / I / want / to / do / something /
good**: In an email from Amazon Alexa titled "Roslyn Or-
lando, Keep Up With Alexa," these phrases were suggested
as "things to try."

45 **the grey curtain**: This phrase is borrowed from the
final page (p. 81) of Mark Fisher's book *Capitalist Realism*
(2009). The "grey curtain" signifies the veil that shrouds
contemporary society in the hegemony of late capitalism,
where we are unable to think beyond its logics or to imag-
ine viable alternative social orders.

50 **Sometimes I dream / of electric sheep**: This
phrase invokes Philip K. Dick's 1968 dystopian sci-fi novel,
Do Androids Dream of Electric Sheep?, and the enduring
question of machines' capacity for empathy and morality.

Acknowledgments

I would like to thank the following people:

Cecilia Flores, for meeting me on the level. Mensah Demary and the Soft Skull team, for tuning in with such exactitude. Terri-ann White, for your vision. Sophy Williams for miraculously finding a way through. Chloe Hooper, for being an early advocate of this manuscript. Stephanie Cobon, for leading me toward poetry. Justin Clemens, for understanding this book's concert with history. Stephen Helper, for your dramaturgy. Blindside Gallery, for giving me the exhibition that led to this book. Ru Moir, for inspiring part one, chapter vii. Raphaelle Moir, for being a new anchor point. Camille Moir, for your love. And Mum, for your echo.

This book was written on the unceded land of the Wurundjeri people of the Kulin Nation. I acknowledge that First Nations peoples are the land's first storytellers. I recognise their continuing connection to land, water, and community and pay my respects to Elders past and present.

ROSLYN ORLANDO is an artist, writer, and gardener based in Melbourne, Australia, on Wurundjeri country. Her writing and artistic works explore relationships among language, history, and technology. She studied journalism at the University of Sydney and arts politics at Tisch School of the Arts at New York University.